MathFlare

Name: _______________________

Class: __________

Teacher: _______________________

Introduction

As parents and educators, we recognize the pivotal role mathematics plays in shaping a child's academic journey and future success. Yet, the path to mathematical proficiency can often seem daunting, fraught with challenges and complexities. That's where the transformative power of MathFlare Workbooks shine through, illuminating the way forward with clarity, precision, and purpose.

Introducing MathFlare Workbooks – a beacon of guidance, a testament to excellence, and a catalyst for achievement. Crafted with meticulous care and expertise, MathFlare Workbooks stand as paragons of educational excellence, designed to nurture young minds, ignite a passion for learning, and develop a deep-rooted understanding of mathematical concepts.

Picture this: your child eagerly delves into the pages of Mathflare Workbook, greeted by a step-by-step guide illuminated with vivid examples that demystify complex mathematical concepts. With each turn of the page, they embark on a journey of discovery, encountering thoughtfully curated practice questions that reinforce learning and hone problem-solving skills. And when they unveil the answers to those very questions, a sense of accomplishment blossoms within them – a tangible reward for their hard work and dedication.

But MathFlare Workbooks are more than just tools for learning; they are pathways to comprehension, fostering a deep-seated understanding of mathematical concepts through a sequential, logical flow. From fundamental principles to advanced problem-solving strategies, every chapter builds upon the last, ensuring a robust foundation upon which future knowledge can be constructed.

As parents, we yearn for nothing more than to see our children thrive, to witness the spark of inspiration ignited within them as they conquer academic challenges with confidence and poise. MathFlare Workbooks serve as partners in this noble endeavor, offering not just practice questions, but the keys to unlocking a world of opportunity.

And for teachers, MathFlare Workbooks stand as invaluable allies in the quest to cultivate mathematical proficiency in the classroom. With answers readily available, instructors can focus on guiding and nurturing their students, confident in the knowledge that MathFlare Workbooks provide a solid framework upon which to build.

In the pages of MathFlare Workbooks, we find not just the promise of academic excellence, but the seeds of a brighter tomorrow. So let us embrace the power of mathematics, let us champion the journey of learning, and let us pave the way for a generation of young minds poised to shape the world. With MathFlare Workbooks as our guide, the possibilities are infinite, and the future, bright.

Table of Contents

MathFlare
MATH WORKBOOK
Grade 2
Step by Step Guide and Essential Practice with Answers
Addition Subtraction
Multiplication
Place Value and Expanded Notations
Geometry
MathFlare Publishing

MathFlare
MATH WORKBOOK
Grade 2-3
Step by Step Guide and Essential Practice with Answers
Addition Subtraction
Multiplication and Division
Place Value and Expanded Notations
Geometry
MathFlare Publishing

MathFlare
MATH WORKBOOK
Grade 3
Step by Step Guide and Essential Practice with Answers
Multiplication and Division
Decimals
Place Value and Expanded Notations
Fractions and Geometry
MathFlare Publishing

MathFlare
MATH WORKBOOK
Grade 1
Step by Step Guide and Essential Practice with Answers
Counting and Numbers
Addition and Subtraction
Place Value and Expanded Notations
Understanding Time
MathFlare Publishing

MathFlare
MATH WORKBOOK
Grade 1-2
Step by Step Guide and Essential Practice with Answers
Counting and Numbers
Addition and Subtraction
Place Value and Expanded Notations
Understanding Time
MathFlare Publishing

MathFlare
MATH WORKBOOK
Grade 3-4
Step by Step Guide and Essential Practice with Answers
Addition Subtraction
Multiplication Division
Place Value and Expanded Notations
Fractions and Geometry
MathFlare Publishing

MathFlare
MATH WORKBOOK
Grade 4
Step by Step Guide and Essential Practice with Answers
Addition Subtraction
Multiplication Division
Place Value and Expanded Notations
Fractions and Geometry
MathFlare Publishing

MathFlare
MATH WORKBOOK
Grade 4-5
Step by Step Guide and Essential Practice with Answers
Multiplication Division
Place Value and Expanded Notations
Fractions and Geometry
Unit Conversion
MathFlare Publishing

MathFlare
Grade 5
MATH WORKBOOK
Step by Step Guide and Essential Practice with Answers
Multiplication Division
Place Value and Expanded Notations
Fractions and Geometry
Unit Conversion
MathFlare Publishing

MathFlare
Grade 5-6
MATH WORKBOOK
Step by Step Guide and Essential Practice with Answers
Multiplication Division
Place Value and Expanded Notations
Fractions and Geometry
Units and Statistics
MathFlare Publishing

MathFlare
Grade 6
MATH WORKBOOK
Step by Step Guide and Essential Practice with Answers
Integers and Statistics
Arithmetic and Pre-Algebra
Fractions and Geometry
Ratio and Percentage
MathFlare Publishing

MathFlare
Grade 6-7
MATH WORKBOOK
Step by Step Guide and Essential Practice with Answers
Arithmetic and Pre-Algebra
Ratio, Percent Proportion
Geometry
Statistics
MathFlare Publishing

MathFlare
Grade 7
MATH WORKBOOK
Step by Step Guide and Essential Practice with Answers
Pre-Algebra
Ratio, Percent Proportion
Geometry
Statistics
MathFlare Publishing

MathFlare
Grade 7-8
MATH WORKBOOK
Step by Step Guide and Essential Practice with Answers
Pre-Algebra
Ratio, Percent Proportion
Geometry and Cartesian Plane
Statistics
MathFlare Publishing

MathFlare
Grade 8-9
MATH WORKBOOK
Step by Step Guide and Essential Practice with Answers
Pre-Algebra
Ratio, Proportion and Percentage
Linear Equations
Geometry and Cartesian Plane
MathFlare Publishing

MathFlare
Grade 8
MATH WORKBOOK
Step by Step Guide and Essential Practice with Answers
Pre-Algebra
Percentage
Linear Equations
Geometry
MathFlare Publishing

Multiplication and Division

Multiplication

Multiplication is an easy way of adding numbers together quickly. Instead of adding the same number repeatedly, we use multiplication to find the total much faster.

For instance, rather than adding 2 + 2 + 2 + 2 + 2, we can multiply 2 by 5 to get the same result: 2 x 5 = 10.

Here, the first number (2) is called the multiplicand, second number (5) is the multiplier. The answer we get, in this case, 10, is called the product.

Let's think of multiplication as repeated addition.

Take 2 x 5, for example. It means adding 2 together five times, which we can illustrate as: 2 + 2 + 2 + 2 + 2 = 10

Multiplication can also be visualized as groups of objects. Imagine we have 2 groups, each containing 5 oranges.

To find the total number of oranges, we multiply the number of groups (2) by the number of oranges in each group (5):

2 groups of 5 oranges = 10 oranges

Expressed as multiplication: 2 x 5 = 10

In summary, multiplication offers various ways to approach it: through repeated addition or by envisioning groups of objects. It's a powerful tool that makes solving math problems much quicker and more efficient!

We can also use the following table to quickly remember multiplication facts. The intersection of two points shows the product of two numbers.

For instance, the product of 5 x 6 = 30, or 6 x 5 = 30.

	1	2	3	4	5	6	7	8	9	10
1	1	2	3	4	5	6	7	8	9	10
2	2	4	6	8	10	12	14	16	18	20
3	3	6	9	12	15	18	21	24	27	30
4	4	8	12	16	20	24	28	32	36	40
5	5	10	15	20	25	30	35	40	45	50
6	6	12	18	24	30	36	42	48	54	60
7	7	14	21	28	35	42	49	56	63	70
8	8	16	24	32	40	48	56	64	72	80
9	9	18	27	36	45	54	63	72	81	90
10	10	20	30	40	50	60	70	80	90	100

<u>Long Division and Remainders</u>

Division is like the opposite of multiplication. It's all about sharing or distributing items equally among a certain number of groups or people.

When we divide one number by another, we're essentially splitting a number into equal parts. We're figuring out how many groups of a certain size can be made from that number.

For instance, let's divide 20 by 4.

When we divide 20 by 4, we're essentially asking, "How many groups of size 4 can we make from 20?"

Now, there are several parts or terms involved in the division process:

- **Dividend:** This is the number being divided, which in this case, is 20.

- **Divisor:** This is the number we're dividing by, which is 4.

- **Quotient:** This is the answer we get after dividing. It tells us how many groups of divisors can be made from the dividend. In this case, the answer is 5.

- **Remainder:** when the divisor doesn't evenly divide the dividend, we get the remainder.

So, when we divide 20 by 4, we found out that 5 groups of 4 can be made from 20.

Let's solve problems from exercises:

```
                              08,464.6
                         10 ) 84,646
                              - 0
                              8 4
                             - 8 0
              8,965 R1          4 6
           9 ) 80,686         - 4 0
             - 72              6 4
               86            - 6 0
             - 81              4 6
               58            - 4 0
             - 54              6 0
               46           - 6 0
             - 45              0
               1
```

Multi Digit Multiplication

```
            93,369
        ×      755
      ___________
    +  4 6 6 8 4 5
    + 4 6 6 8 4 5
    + 6 5 3 5 8 3
    ___________
    = 7 0 4 9 3 5 9 5
    ___________
```

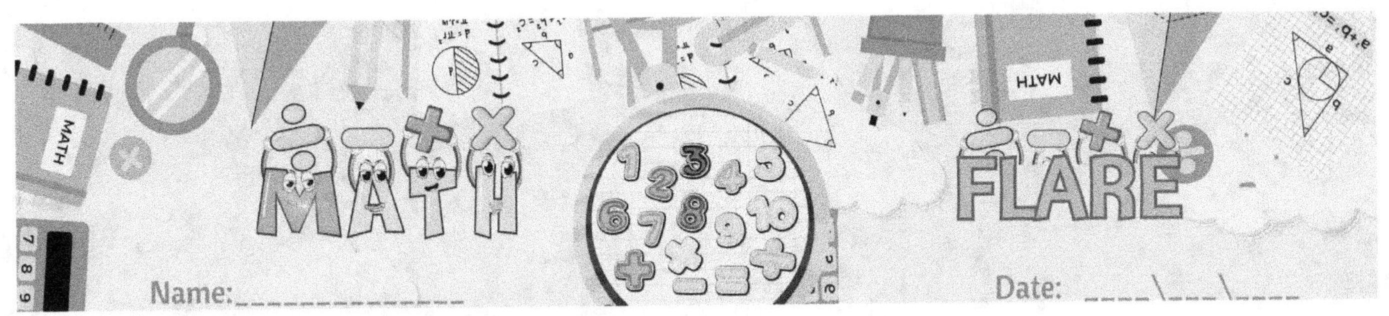

Multi Digit Multiplication

Find the product.

1. 36,771
   ×   552

2. 48,973
   ×   972

3. 55,447
   ×   149

4. 68,356
   ×   134

5. 51,386
   ×   189

6. 24,667
   ×   734

7. 16,878
   ×   874

8. 29,353
   ×   778

9. 96,030
   ×   162

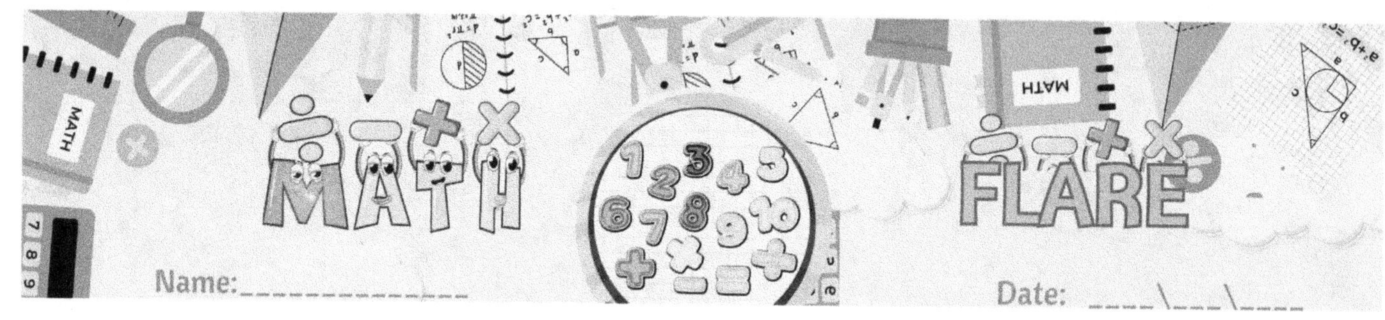

10. 86,185
× 952

11. 56,460
× 673

12. 80,224
× 557

13. 66,354
× 812

14. 66,424
× 785

15. 82,165
× 631

16. 26,678
× 195

17. 19,774
× 352

18. 20,199
× 163

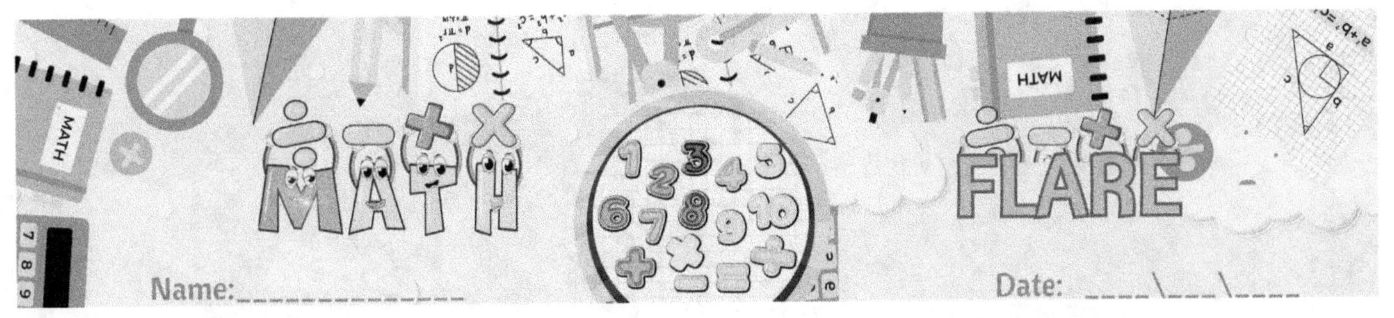

19.   59,935
   ×   940

20.   47,538
   ×   609

21.   57,965
   ×   212

22.   42,689
   ×   305

23.   30,744
   ×   129

24.   67,556
   ×   191

25.   59,977
   ×   697

26.   42,578
   ×   623

27.   85,230
   ×   385

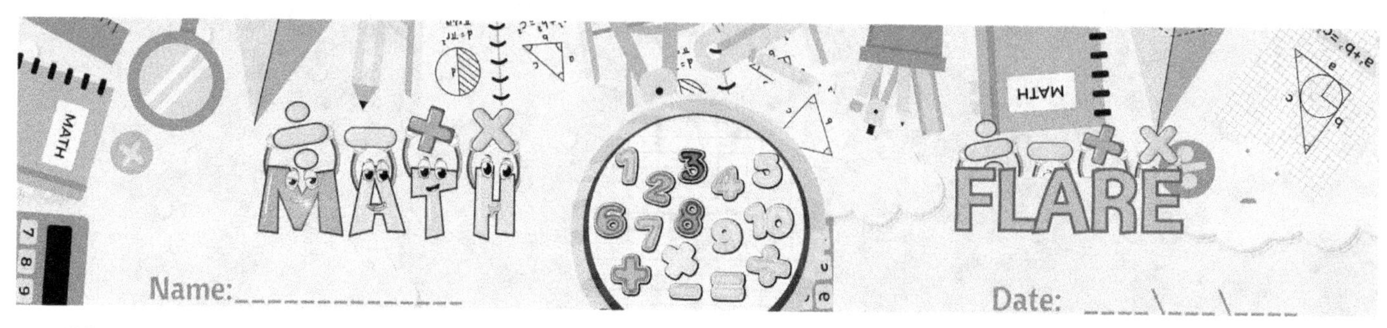

28. 61,037
× 693

29. 75,022
× 931

30. 40,887
× 741

31. 48,486
× 897

32. 31,184
× 882

33. 92,221
× 151

34. 63,646
× 815

35. 77,292
× 231

36. 27,975
× 119

MathFlare - Multiplication and Division 5th Grade

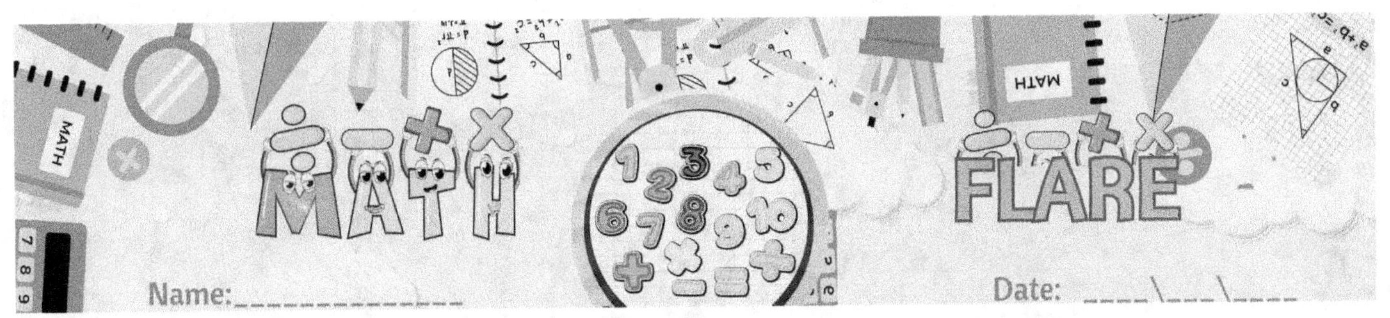

37. 68,682
× 352

38. 47,360
× 453

39. 34,666
× 597

40. 35,032
× 634

41. 23,743
× 572

42. 28,631
× 224

43. 30,552
× 642

44. 34,319
× 812

45. 74,200
× 507

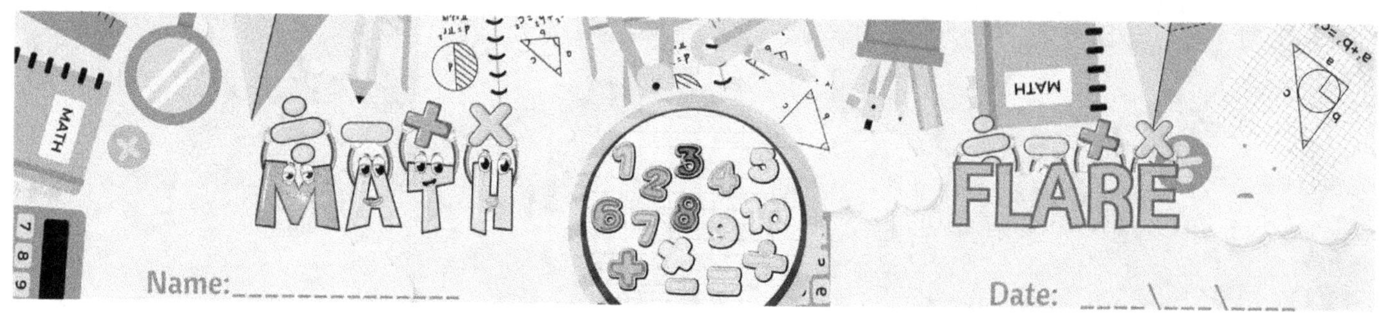

46.
$$41{,}226 \times 667$$

47.
$$63{,}246 \times 733$$

48.
$$22{,}463 \times 682$$

49.
$$89{,}980 \times 544$$

50.
$$38{,}244 \times 256$$

51.
$$49{,}218 \times 858$$

52.
$$41{,}843 \times 468$$

53.
$$51{,}795 \times 407$$

54.
$$93{,}695 \times 599$$

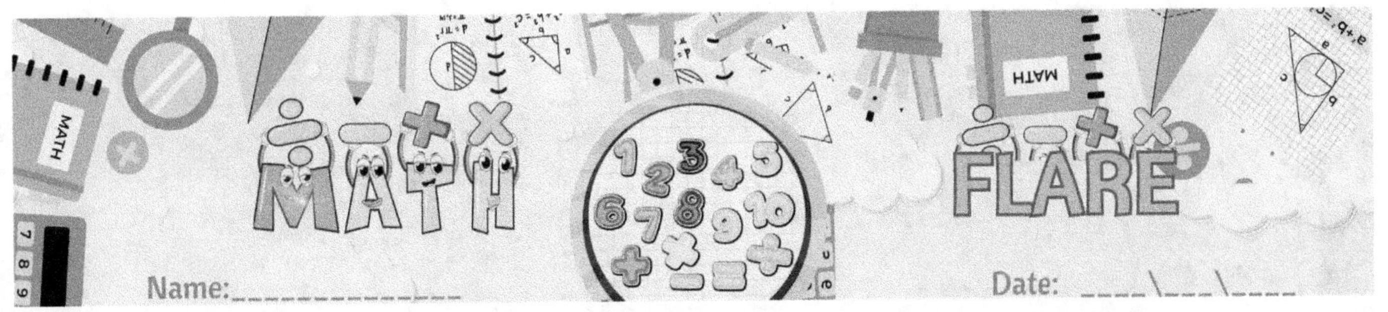

55.   91,126
×   257

56.   44,740
×   253

57.   68,155
×   773

58.   60,394
×   911

59.   71,107
×   188

60.   67,694
×   379

61.   80,779
×   823

62.   17,422
×   365

63.   81,858
×   612

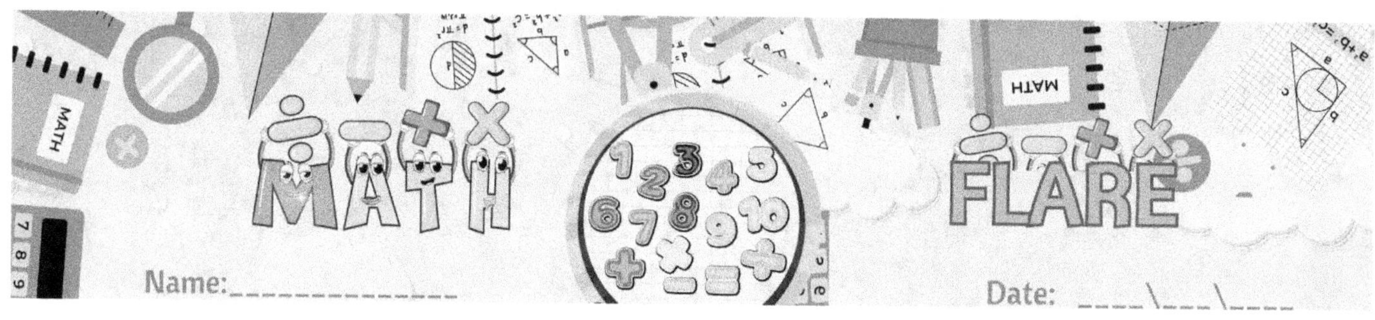

Long Division
Find the quotient.

64.

$13\overline{)59{,}471}$

65.

$20\overline{)36{,}477}$

66.

$9\overline{)40{,}752}$

67.

$2\overline{)60{,}918}$

68.

$4\overline{)62{,}350}$

69.

$18\overline{)92{,}792}$

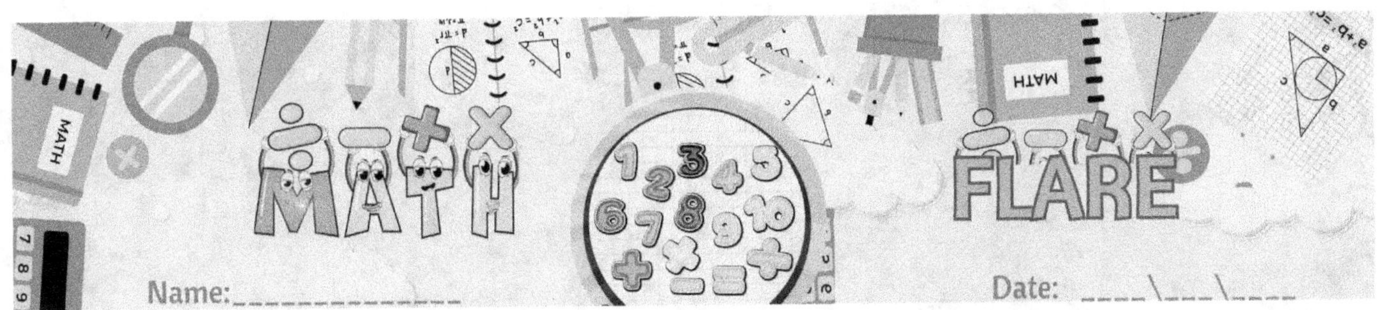

70.

$$5 \overline{)\ 51{,}975}$$

71.

$$19 \overline{)\ 36{,}282}$$

72.

$$3 \overline{)\ 52{,}893}$$

73.

$$8 \overline{)\ 18{,}790}$$

74.

$$18 \overline{)\ 29{,}046}$$

75.

$$10 \overline{)\ 96{,}784}$$

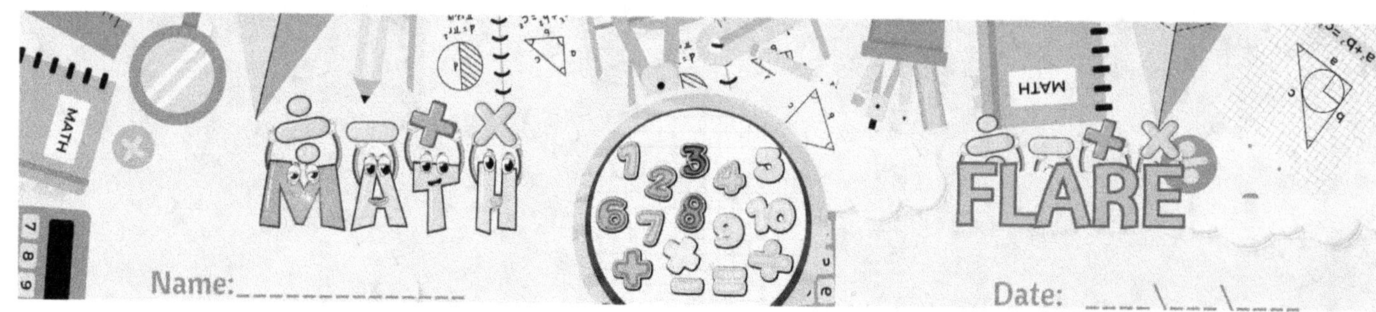

76.

$$8\overline{)17{,}471}$$

77.

$$7\overline{)51{,}882}$$

78.

$$2\overline{)47{,}656}$$

79.

$$16\overline{)21{,}806}$$

80.

$$17\overline{)69{,}175}$$

81.

$$4\overline{)72{,}344}$$

82.

$$7 \overline{)\, 56{,}041}$$

83.

$$8 \overline{)\, 63{,}326}$$

84.

$$19 \overline{)\, 66{,}623}$$

85.

$$10 \overline{)\, 31{,}241}$$

86.

$$14 \overline{)\, 97{,}282}$$

87.

$$16 \overline{)\, 75{,}517}$$

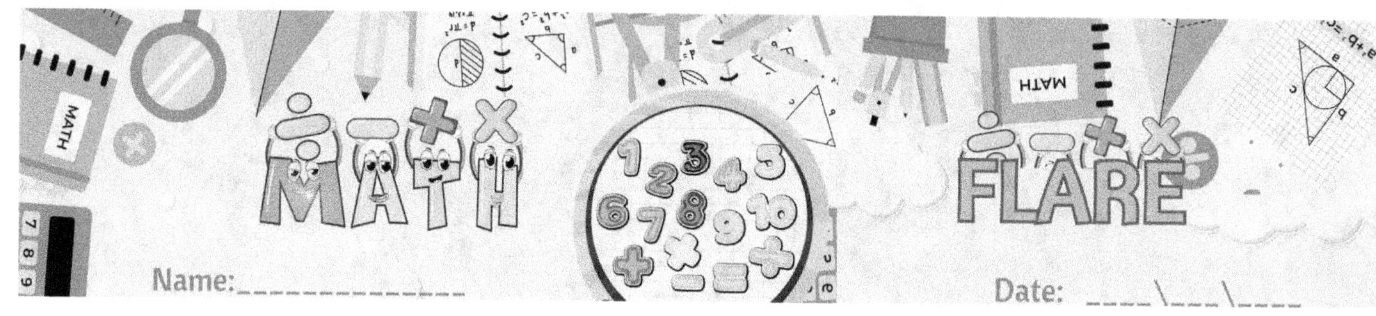

88.

$18\overline{)34{,}758}$

89.

$3\overline{)36{,}380}$

90.

$8\overline{)72{,}493}$

91.

$14\overline{)66{,}993}$

92.

$17\overline{)66{,}712}$

93.

$3\overline{)91{,}517}$

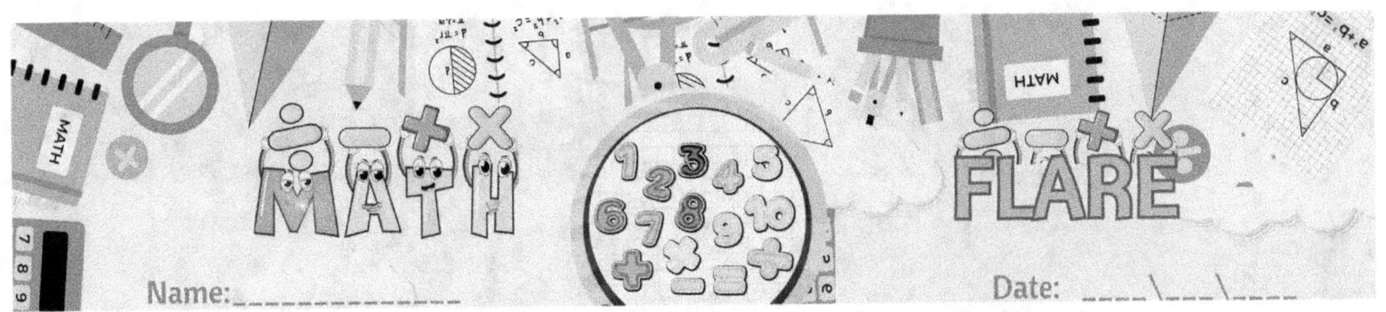

94.

$$7 \overline{) 91{,}927}$$

95.

$$12 \overline{) 62{,}980}$$

96.

$$4 \overline{) 99{,}307}$$

97.

$$14 \overline{) 29{,}848}$$

98.

$$6 \overline{) 54{,}978}$$

99.

$$5 \overline{) 47{,}340}$$

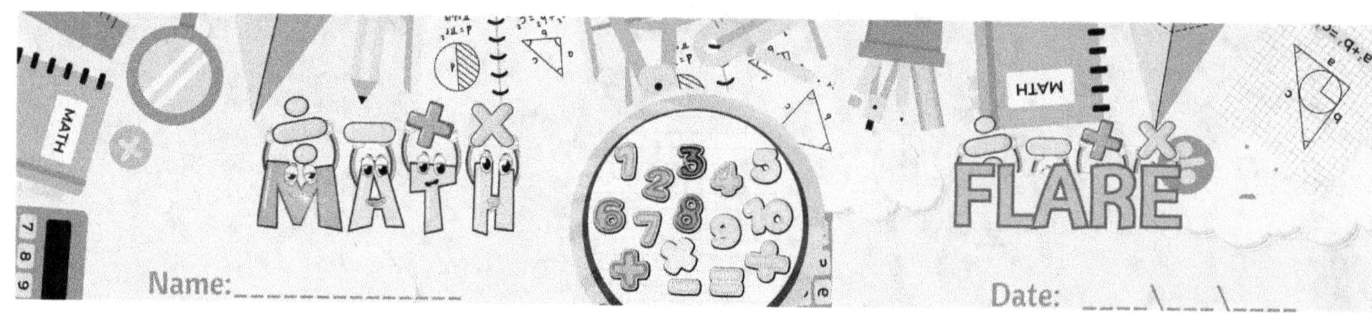

100.

$$15 \overline{)\,51{,}019}$$

101.

$$7 \overline{)\,73{,}065}$$

102.

$$12 \overline{)\,69{,}929}$$

103.

$$10 \overline{)\,51{,}832}$$

104.

$$14 \overline{)\,62{,}670}$$

105.

$$11 \overline{)\,11{,}342}$$

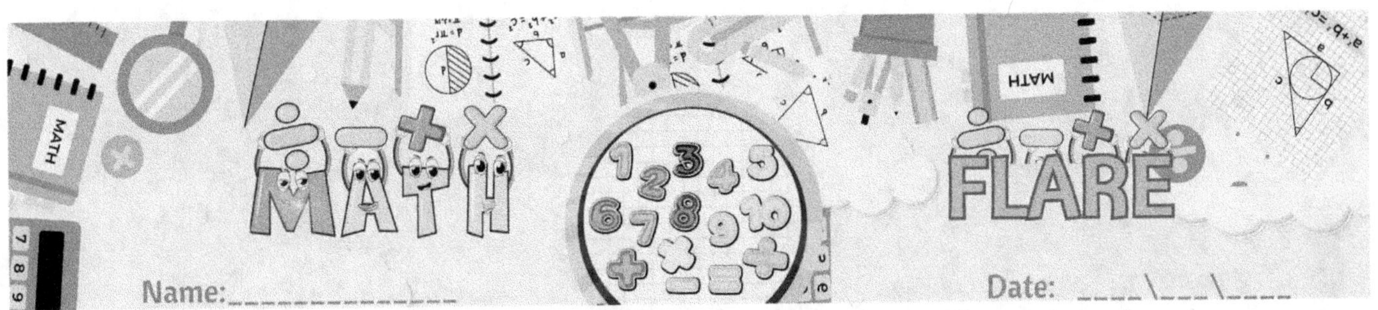

106.

4$\overline{)75{,}524}$

107.

8$\overline{)18{,}453}$

108.

3$\overline{)26{,}404}$

109.

14$\overline{)51{,}488}$

110.

12$\overline{)45{,}905}$

111.

8$\overline{)49{,}574}$

MathFlare - Multiplication and Division 5th Grade

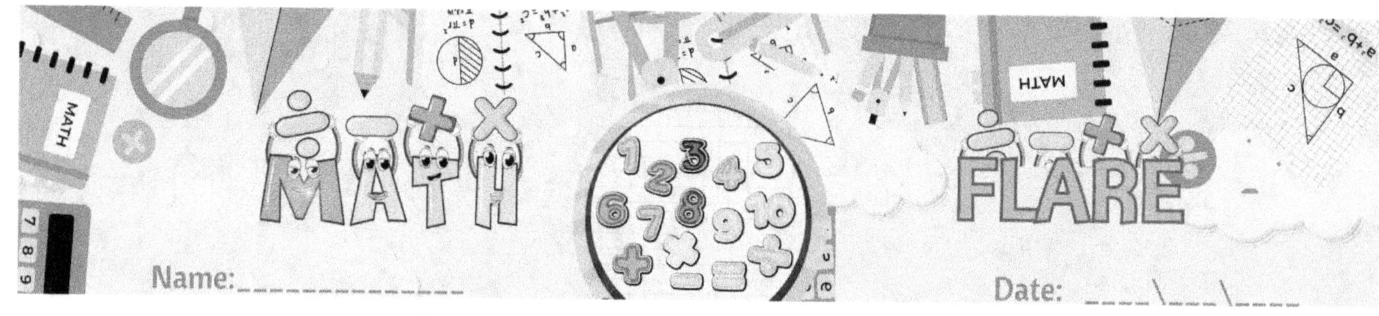

Long Division: Remainders

Find the quotient.

112.

$$42 \overline{)\,891{,}572}$$

113.

$$19 \overline{)\,449{,}300}$$

114.

$$49 \overline{)\,240{,}184}$$

115.

$$45 \overline{)\,698{,}284}$$

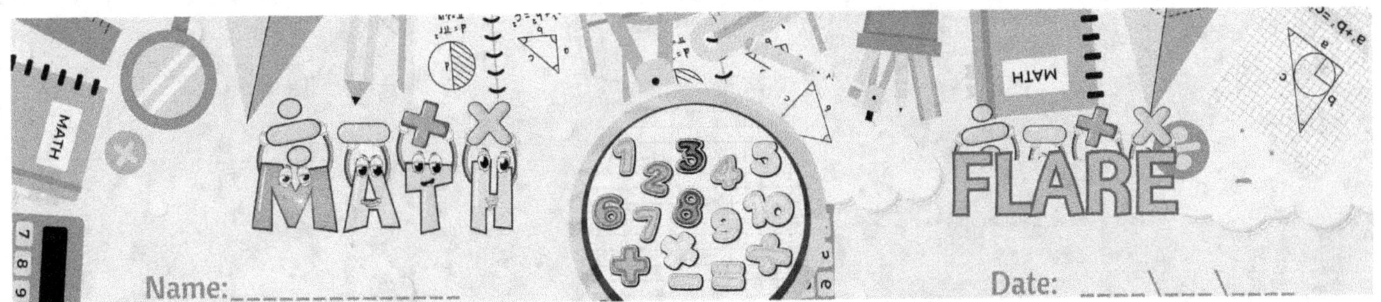

116.

$$33\overline{)769{,}356}$$

117.

$$47\overline{)280{,}471}$$

118.

$$47\overline{)504{,}866}$$

119.

$$31\overline{)965{,}184}$$

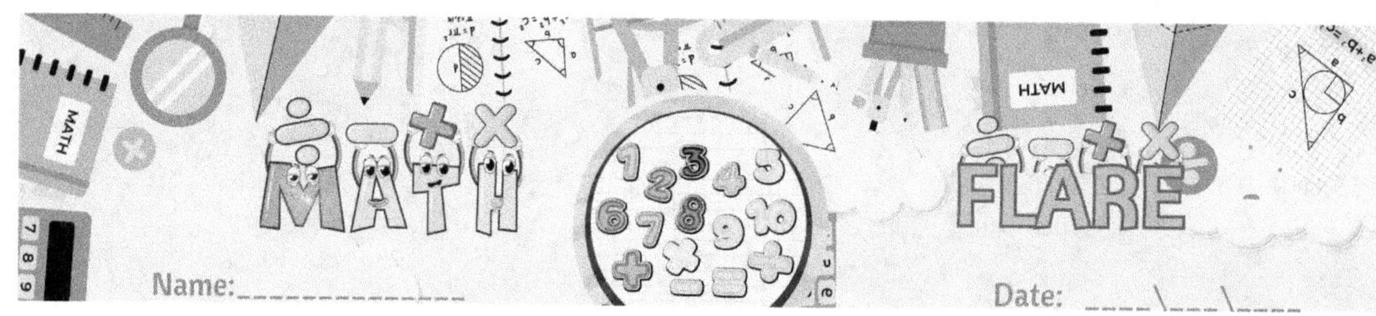

120.

$$12\overline{)259{,}911}$$

121.

$$50\overline{)835{,}747}$$

122.

$$28\overline{)837{,}765}$$

123.

$$15\overline{)972{,}717}$$

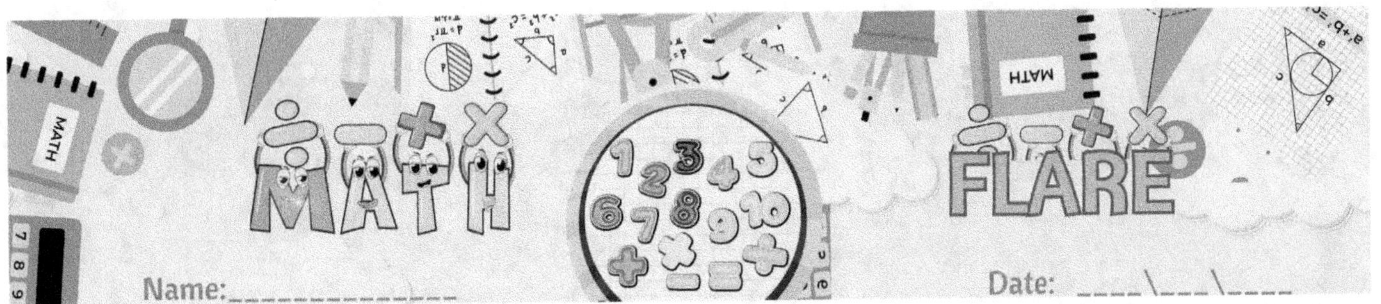

124.

$$21 \overline{)\ 576,440}$$

125.

$$48 \overline{)\ 129,169}$$

126.

$$45 \overline{)\ 759,960}$$

127.

$$12 \overline{)\ 906,429}$$

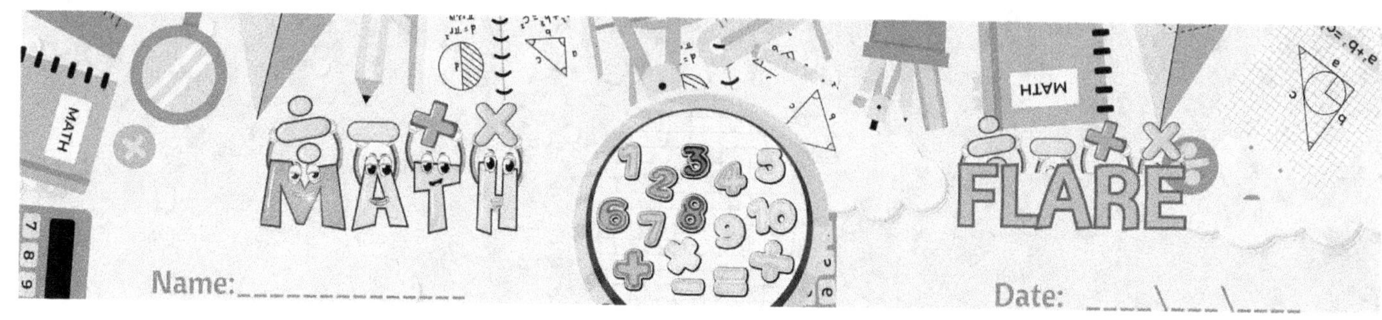

128.

21) 193,609

129.

18) 491,302

130.

45) 674,091

131.

20) 958,476

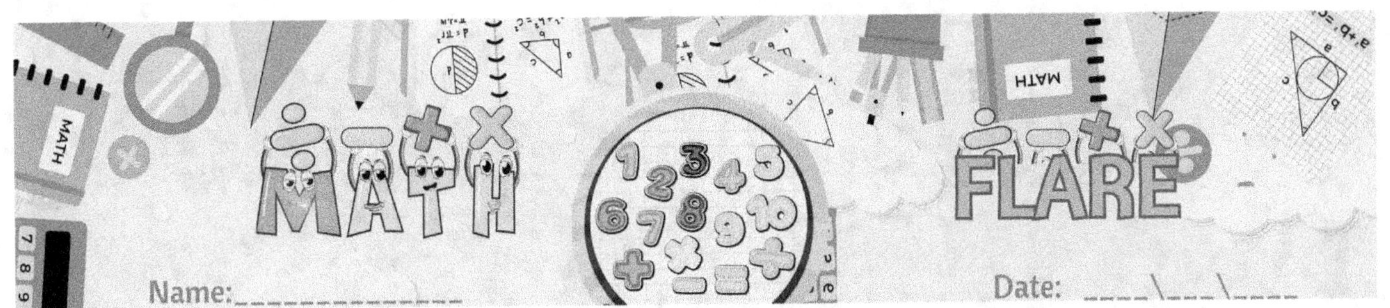

132.

$$41 \overline{) 465,766}$$

133.

$$12 \overline{) 506,951}$$

134.

$$22 \overline{) 285,957}$$

135.

$$17 \overline{) 138,992}$$

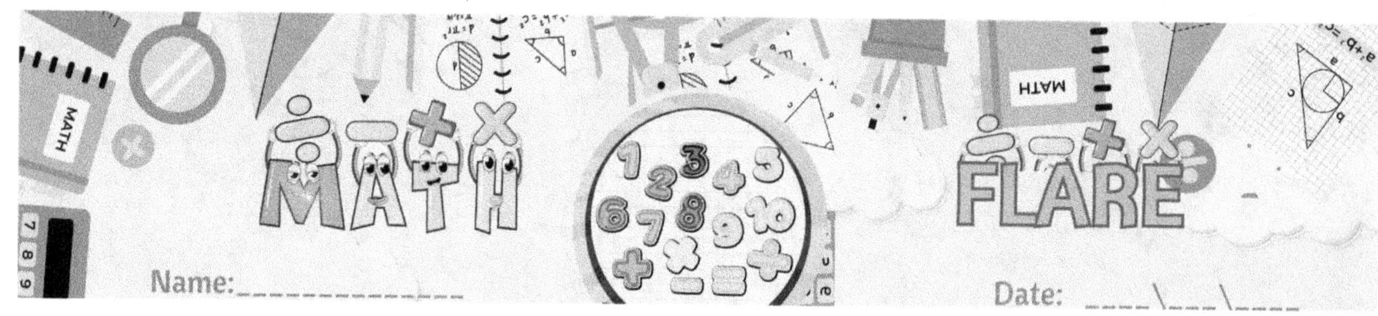

136.

$$48\overline{)152{,}103}$$

137.

$$26\overline{)986{,}552}$$

138.

$$27\overline{)917{,}549}$$

139.

$$27\overline{)246{,}573}$$

140.

21) 850,783

141.

45) 735,907

142.

38) 945,627

143.

45) 232,849

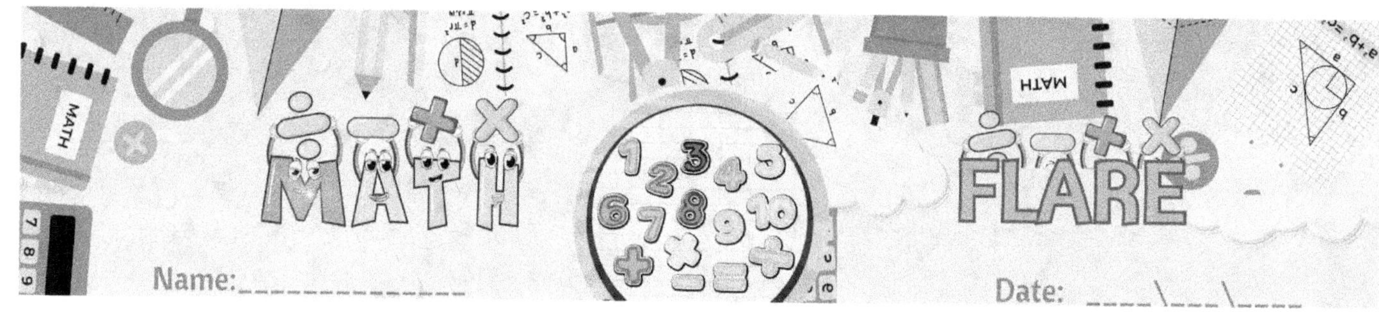

144.

$$16 \overline{)716{,}731}$$

145.

$$17 \overline{)843{,}246}$$

146.

$$40 \overline{)530{,}374}$$

147.

$$22 \overline{)894{,}860}$$

148.

$$33\overline{)177{,}918}$$

149.

$$12\overline{)623{,}068}$$

150.

$$47\overline{)102{,}080}$$

151.

$$20\overline{)922{,}769}$$

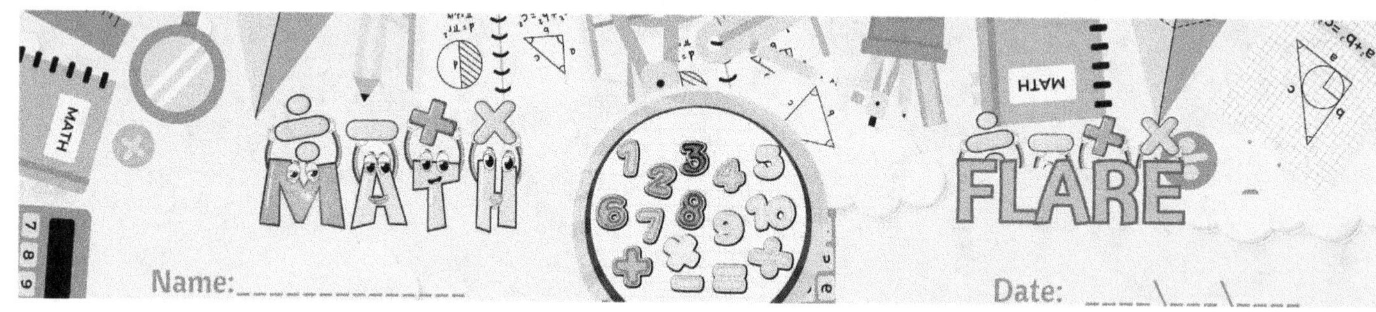

152.

$$44 \overline{)310{,}317}$$

153.

$$41 \overline{)910{,}558}$$

154.

$$30 \overline{)891{,}655}$$

155.

$$37 \overline{)226{,}125}$$

156.

$$10 \overline{)\ 203{,}465}$$

157.

$$25 \overline{)\ 430{,}882}$$

158.

$$13 \overline{)\ 259{,}394}$$

159.

$$38 \overline{)\ 373{,}677}$$

160.

$$33 \overline{)666{,}926}$$

161.

$$12 \overline{)433{,}967}$$

162.

$$45 \overline{)516{,}602}$$

163.

$$22 \overline{)731{,}684}$$

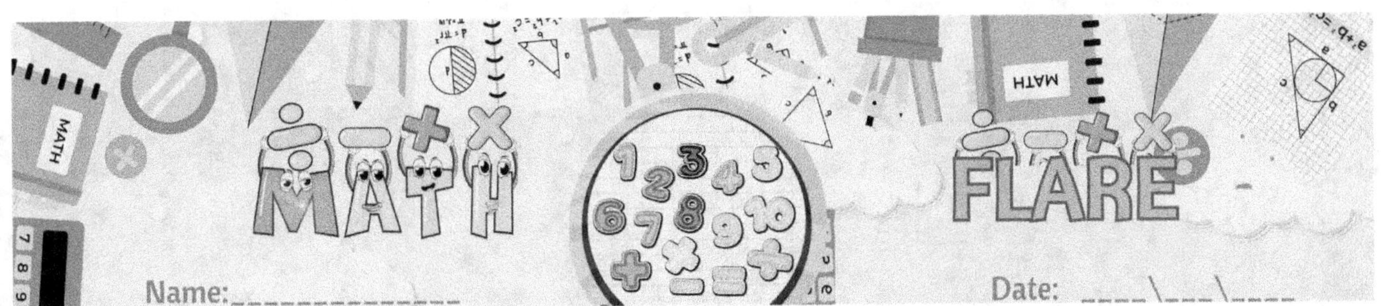

164.

$$38 \overline{)158{,}717}$$

165.

$$23 \overline{)377{,}424}$$

166.

$$15 \overline{)869{,}368}$$

167.

$$47 \overline{)480{,}462}$$

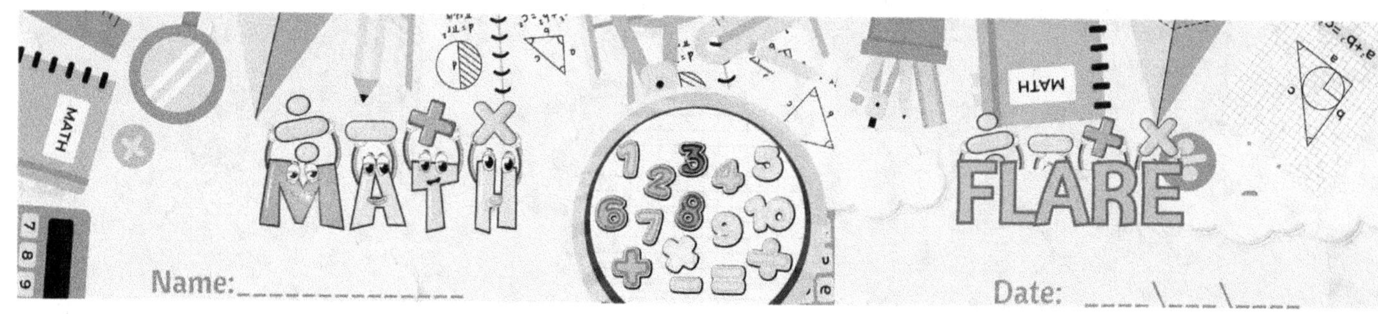

168.

$$29\overline{)417,804}$$

169.

$$13\overline{)680,557}$$

170.

$$25\overline{)825,063}$$

171.

$$17\overline{)999,492}$$

172.

$$16 \overline{)\ 110{,}671}$$

173.

$$29 \overline{)\ 151{,}363}$$

174.

$$31 \overline{)\ 452{,}636}$$

175.

$$10 \overline{)\ 205{,}215}$$

176.

$$45 \overline{)\ 342{,}764}$$

177.

$$27 \overline{)\ 471{,}063}$$

178.

$$44 \overline{)\ 588{,}051}$$

179.

$$24 \overline{)\ 799{,}988}$$

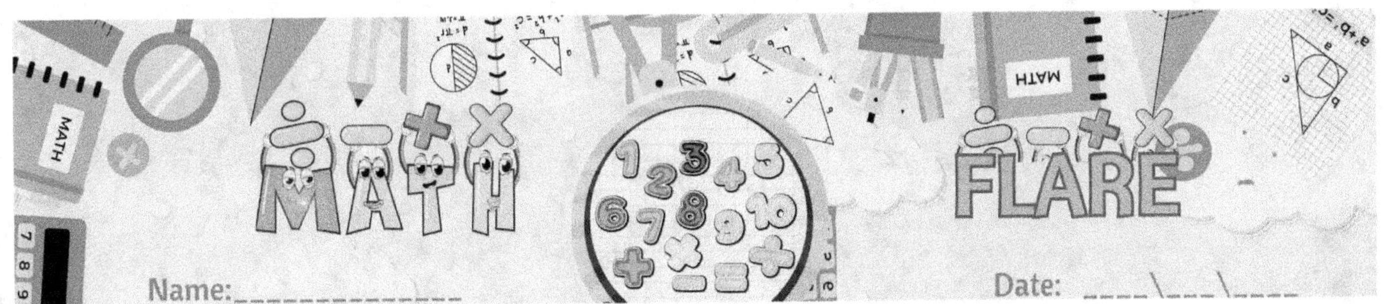

180.

$$34\overline{)235{,}425}$$

181.

$$18\overline{)747{,}665}$$

182.

$$42\overline{)273{,}664}$$

183.

$$50\overline{)831{,}801}$$

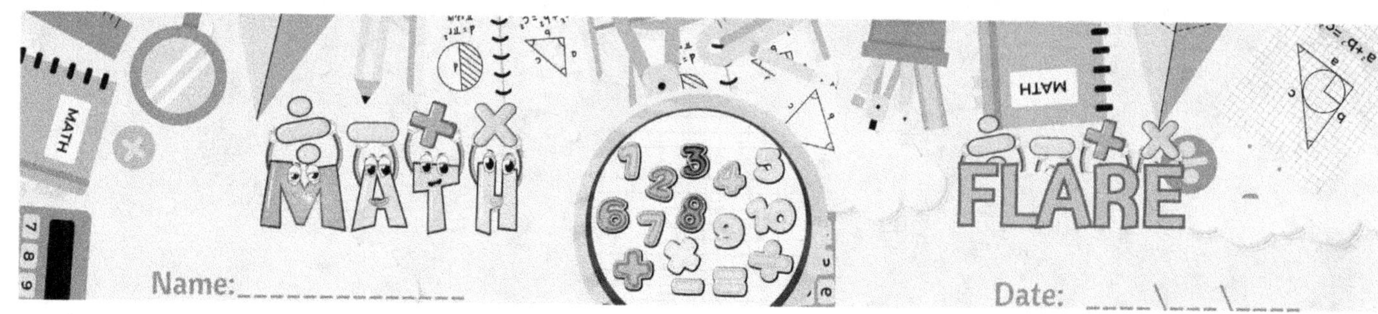

184.

$$28 \overline{)\ 628{,}298}$$

185.

$$38 \overline{)\ 115{,}714}$$

186.

$$19 \overline{)\ 487{,}044}$$

187.

$$21 \overline{)\ 905{,}079}$$

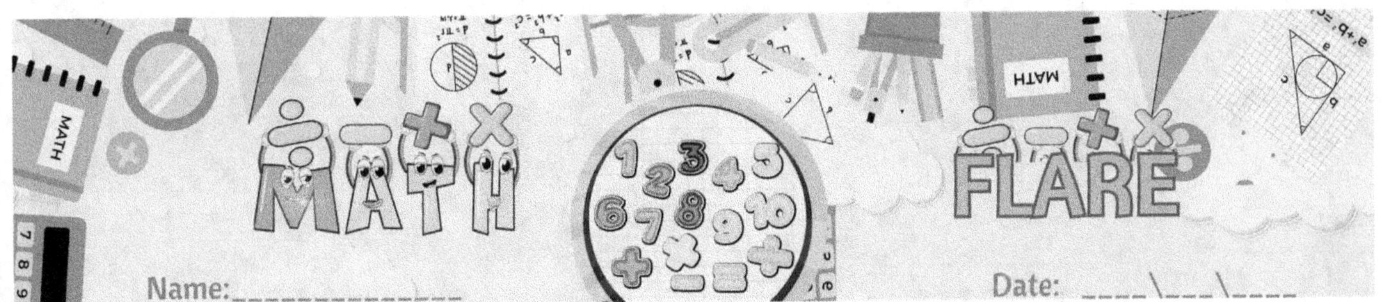

188.

$$17 \overline{)616{,}310}$$

189.

$$22 \overline{)138{,}489}$$

190.

$$19 \overline{)832{,}800}$$

191.

$$32 \overline{)915{,}946}$$

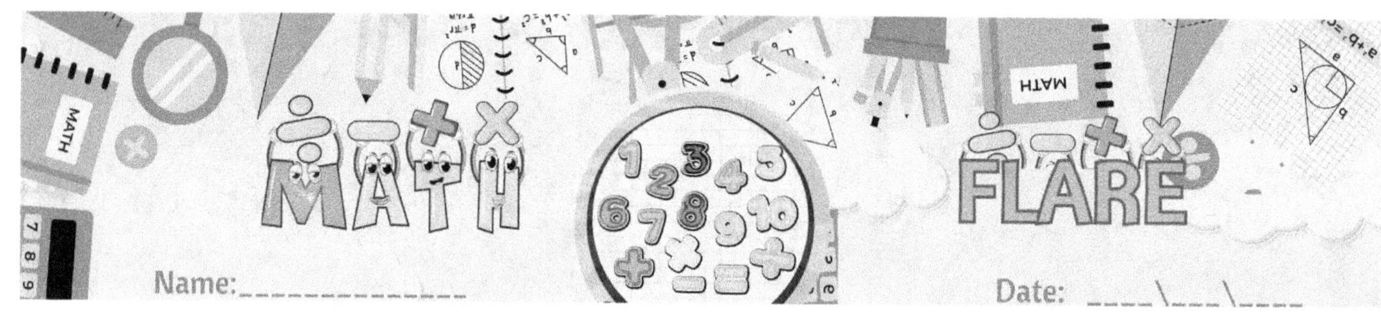

Using the Power of 10

192.
$$8,000 \times 0.01$$

193.
$$9,000 \times 0.1$$

194.
$$3,000 \times 0.1$$

195.
$$10\overline{)3,000}$$

196.
$$0.1\overline{)9,000}$$

197.
$$0.01\overline{)2,000}$$

198.
$$3,000 \times 0.01$$

199.
$$100\overline{)7,000}$$

200.
$$6,000 \times 0.1$$

201.
$$100\overline{)7,000}$$

202.
$$5,000 \times 10$$

203.
$$0.1\overline{)8,000}$$

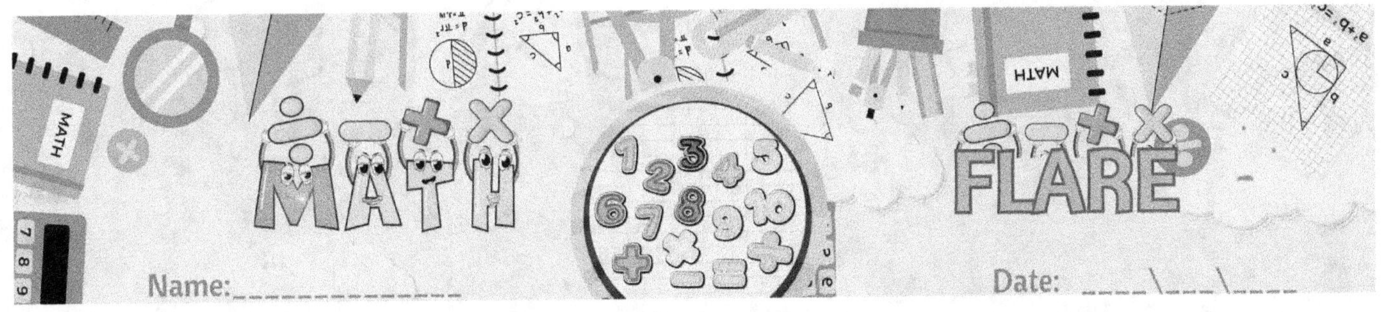

204.

$$1{,}000 \overline{)\,1{,}000}$$

205.

$$0.01 \overline{)\,6{,}000}$$

206.

$$0.01 \overline{)\,2{,}000}$$

207.

$$\begin{array}{r} 9{,}000 \\ \times\ \ 1{,}000 \\ \hline \end{array}$$

208.

$$1{,}000 \overline{)\,2{,}000}$$

209.

$$\begin{array}{r} 4{,}000 \\ \times\ \ \ \ \ 10 \\ \hline \end{array}$$

210.

$$\begin{array}{r} 1{,}000 \\ \times\ \ \ \ 100 \\ \hline \end{array}$$

211.

$$\begin{array}{r} 1{,}000 \\ \times\ \ 1{,}000 \\ \hline \end{array}$$

212.

$$\begin{array}{r} 3{,}000 \\ \times\ \ \ 0.01 \\ \hline \end{array}$$

213.

$$100 \overline{)\,5{,}000}$$

214.

$$\begin{array}{r} 4{,}000 \\ \times\ \ \ \ 0.1 \\ \hline \end{array}$$

215.

$$0.01 \overline{)\,4{,}000}$$

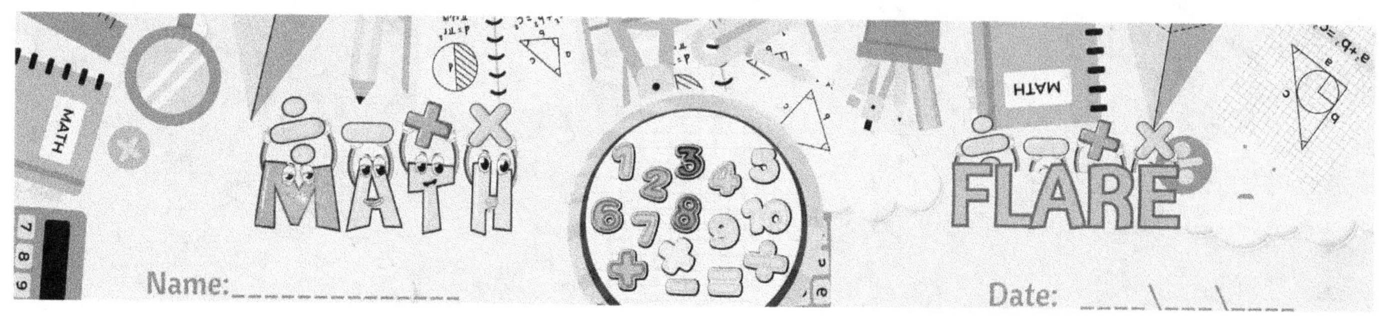

216.
$$6{,}000 \times 0.01$$

217.
$$9{,}000 \times 100$$

218.
$$100 \overline{)\,5{,}000}$$

219.
$$5{,}000 \times 0.1$$

220.
$$7{,}000 \times 1{,}000$$

221.
$$1{,}000 \overline{)\,7{,}000}$$

222.
$$6{,}000 \times 0.01$$

223.
$$7{,}000 \times 10$$

224.
$$8{,}000 \times 1{,}000$$

225.
$$9{,}000 \times 1{,}000$$

226.
$$0.01 \overline{)\,3{,}000}$$

227.
$$100 \overline{)\,9{,}000}$$

228.

$$0.1 \overline{)3{,}000}$$

229.

$$10 \overline{)4{,}000}$$

230.

$$\begin{array}{r} 1{,}000 \\ \times \quad 0.1 \\ \hline \end{array}$$

231.

$$\begin{array}{r} 5{,}000 \\ \times \quad 0.01 \\ \hline \end{array}$$

232.

$$\begin{array}{r} 6{,}000 \\ \times \quad 0.01 \\ \hline \end{array}$$

233.

$$0.01 \overline{)7{,}000}$$

234.

$$0.1 \overline{)6{,}000}$$

235.

$$0.01 \overline{)1{,}000}$$

236.

$$0.1 \overline{)9{,}000}$$

237.

$$10 \overline{)4{,}000}$$

238.

$$\begin{array}{r} 1{,}000 \\ \times \quad 0.01 \\ \hline \end{array}$$

239.

$$\begin{array}{r} 5{,}000 \\ \times \quad 100 \\ \hline \end{array}$$

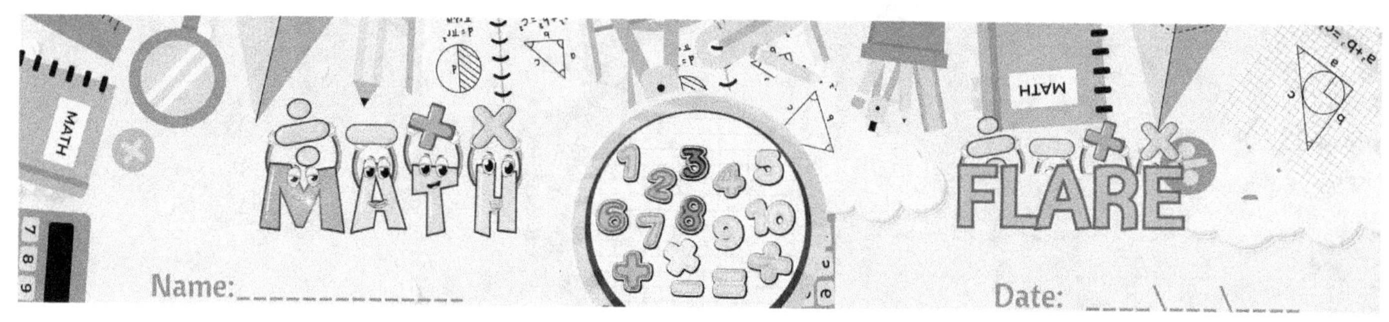

240. $4{,}000 \times 10$

241. $8{,}000 \times 10$

242. $3{,}000 \times 1{,}000$

243. $4{,}000 \times 100$

244. $0.01\overline{)7{,}000}$

245. $2{,}000 \times 100$

246. $100\overline{)4{,}000}$

247. $0.1\overline{)3{,}000}$

248. $0.01\overline{)5{,}000}$

249. $0.1\overline{)8{,}000}$

250. $10\overline{)6{,}000}$

251. $10\overline{)9{,}000}$

Multiplication Word Problems

252. Oliver can catch 13 fish per hour. How many fish can Oliver catch in four hours?

253. Violet wants to make four flower arrangements, and each arrangement requires 14 flowers. How many flowers does Violet need in total?

254. Nova baked nine batches of cookies. Each batch had two cookies. How many cookies did Nova bake in all?

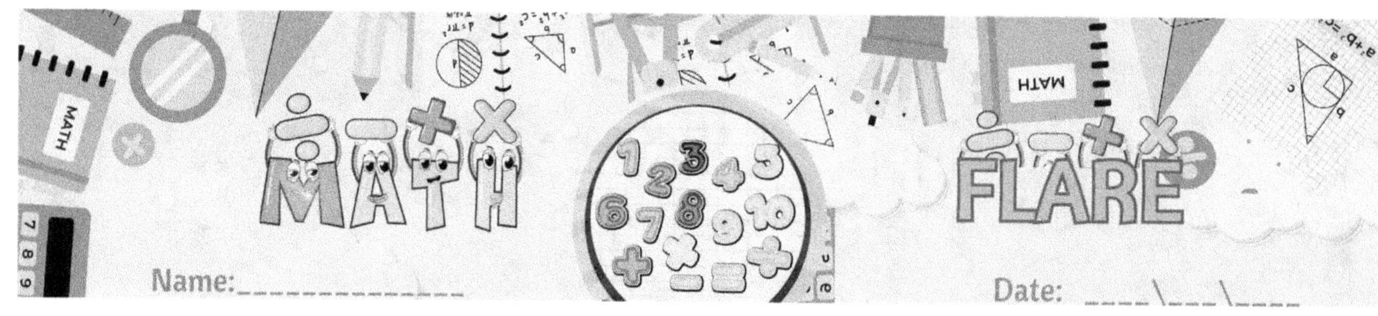

255. A box contains 12 bottles of juice, and each bottle contains 19 ounces of juice. How many ounces of juice are there in total?

256. Ariana has 18 boxes of combs. Each box has 14 combs. How many combs does Ariana have in all?

257. A movie theater can seat six people. How many people can it seat in 13 showings?

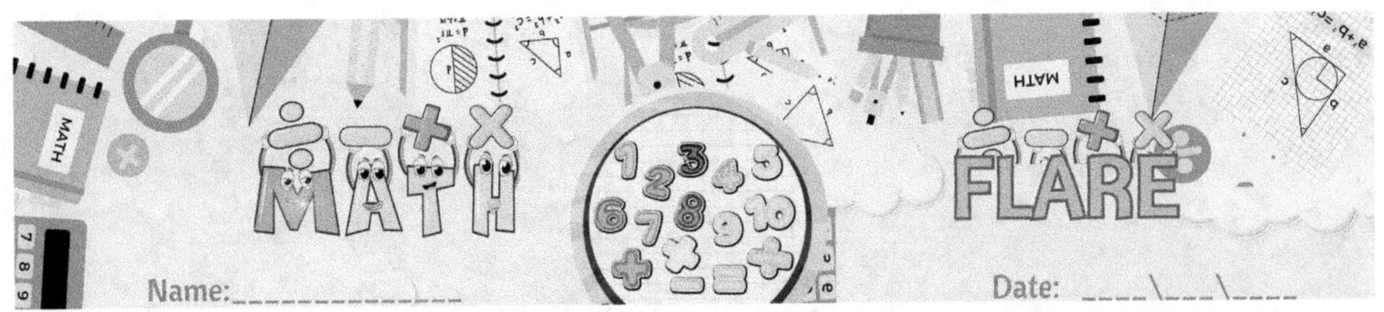

258. Zachary can run 18 laps in 1 hour. How many laps can Zachary run in 11 hour?

259. If a car travels at four miles per hour for 19 hours, how far will it go?

260. Aria baked 13 batches of cakes. Each batch had 17 cakes. How many cakes did Aria bake in all?

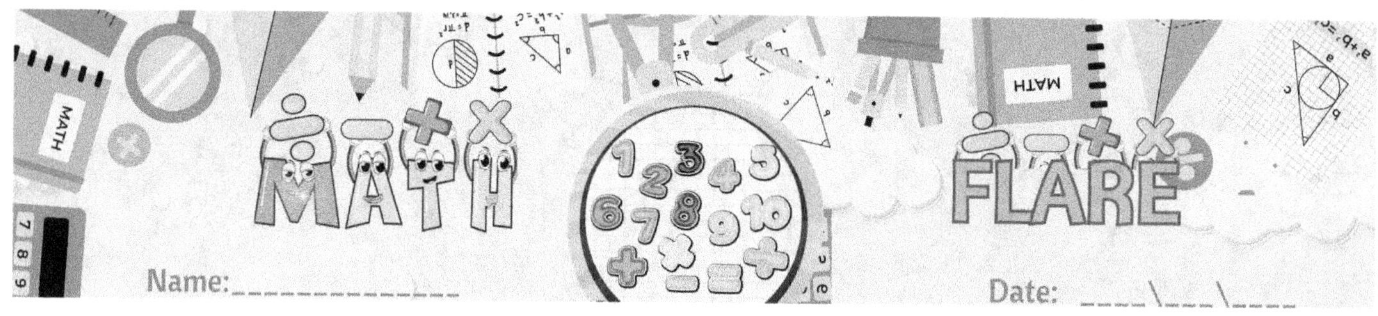

261. Maria has five vases of flowers. Each vase has 10 flowers. How many flowers does Maria have in all?

262. Madeline has nine yards of fabric, and each dress requires 20 yards of fabric. How many dresses can Madeline make?

263. Micah can solve seven math problems in one hour. How many math problems can Micah solve in 12 hours?

264. If a train travels at two miles per hour for 13 hours, how far will it go?

265. If there are 12 students in each classroom and there are 15 classrooms, how many students are there in total?

266. If a boat travels at 19 miles per hour for eight hours, how far will it go?

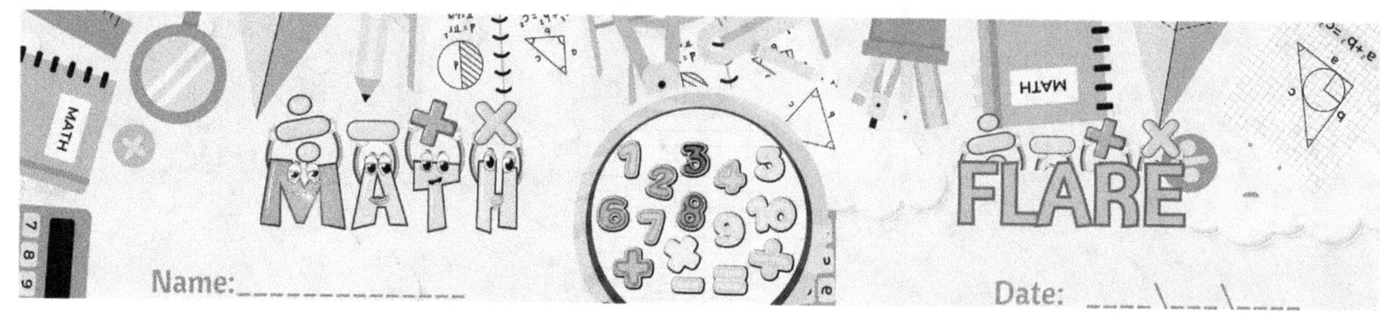

267. Chase can type eight words per minute. How many words can Chase type in two minutes?

268. Xavier can make 18 sandwiches in 1 hour. How many sandwiches can he make in six hour?

269. Kaylee has six jars of jam. Each jar has 18 ounces of jam. How many ounces of jam does Kaylee have in all?

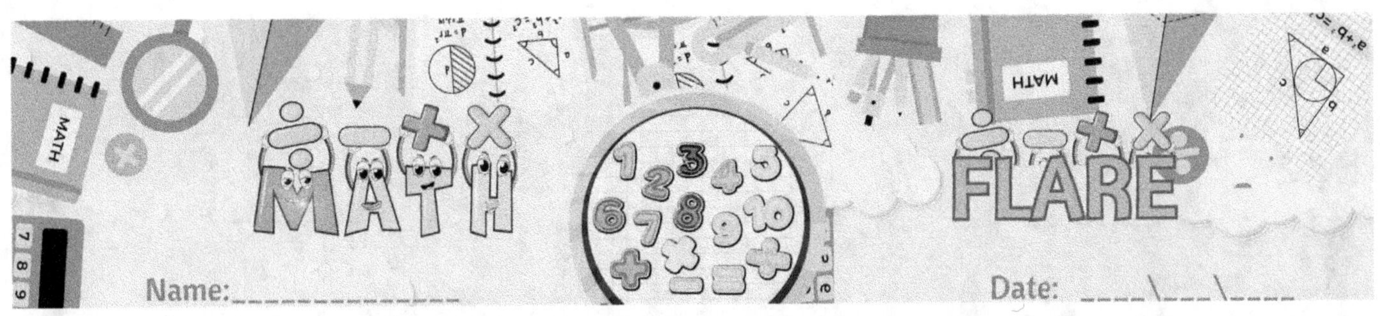

270. There are 17 students in a class. If each student needs three pencils, how many pencils are needed for the class in total?

271. If Isaac can paint 12 square feet of wall in one hour, how many square feet of wall can he paint in 15 hours?

272. Jayden can solve 19 math problems in one hour. How many problems can Jayden solve in 20 hours?

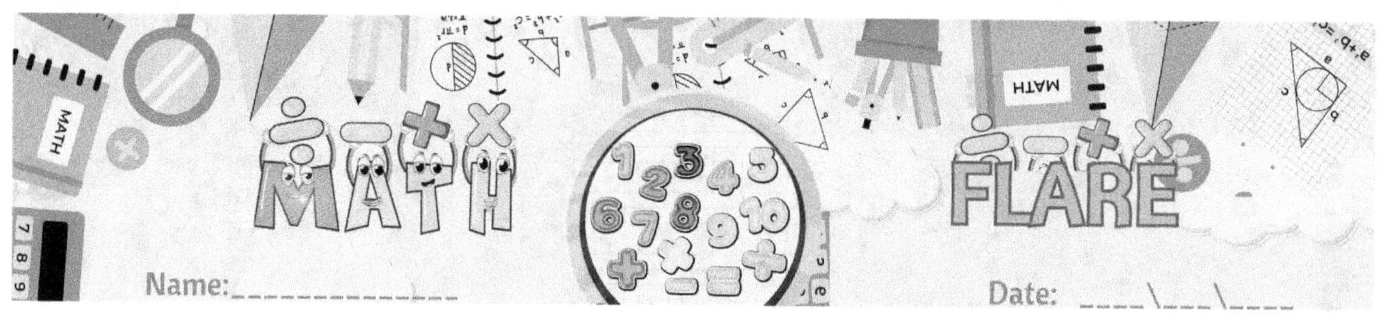

273. There are 11 pencils in each pack. If Gabriella buys 17 packs, how many pencils will Gabriella have?

274. There are seven slices of pizza in each box. If Hazel orders nine boxes, how many slices of pizza will Hazel have?

275. Jason can ride 10 miles in one hour. How far can he ride in 11 hours?

276. Chloe has seven containers of paint. Each container holds seven liters of paint. How many liters of paint does Chloe have in total?

277. Michael runs two miles every day. How many miles will Michael run in five days?

278. Wyatt sells 13 cakes each day at his bakery. If he works three days, how many cakes does he sell?

279. Owen earns three dollars per hour. How much will Owen earn after working for 13 hours?

280. There are 17 pages in a book. If 13 books are needed for a class, how many pages are there in total?

281. Hudson runs 13 miles per week. How many miles will Hudson run in 16 weeks?

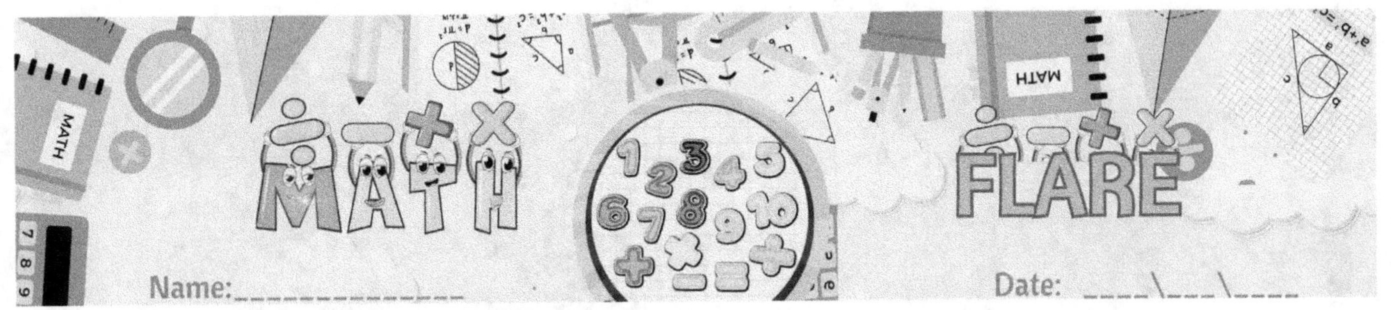

Division Word Problems

282. A book has 870 chapters. If you want to read the book in 10 days, how many chapters do you need to read per day?

283. A car can travel 1,040 miles on 20 gallons of gas. How many miles can it travel on 1 gallon of gas?

284. Willow has 216 cookies and wants to divide them equally into eight bags. How many cookies will be in each bag?

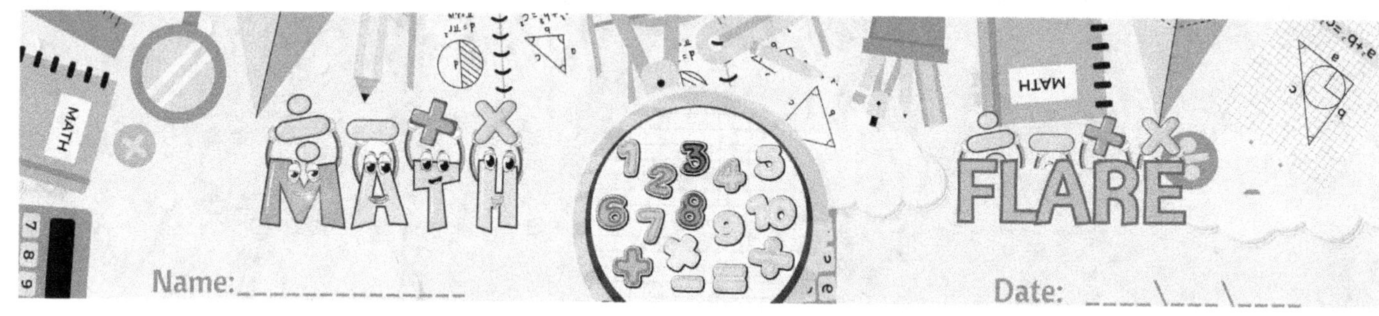

285. Chase scored 1,056 points in 16 games. What is his average score per game?

286. At a restaurant, seven friends decided to divide the bill equally. If each person paid $27, then what was the total bill?

287. It takes Genesis 55 minutes to write 1 page. How many pages can Genesis write in 165 minutes?

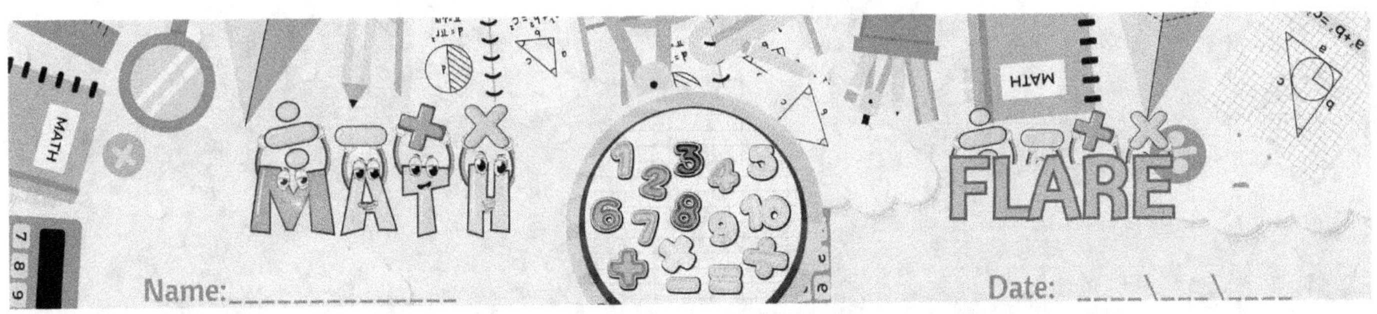

288. A box contains 282 candy bars. If each candy bar has six calories, how many calories are there in the box?

289. If Lily has 516 combs and wants to distribute them equally to 12 students, how many combs will each student get?

290. Chloe has $470 and she wants to buy 10 brushes that cost the same amount. How much does each brushes cost?

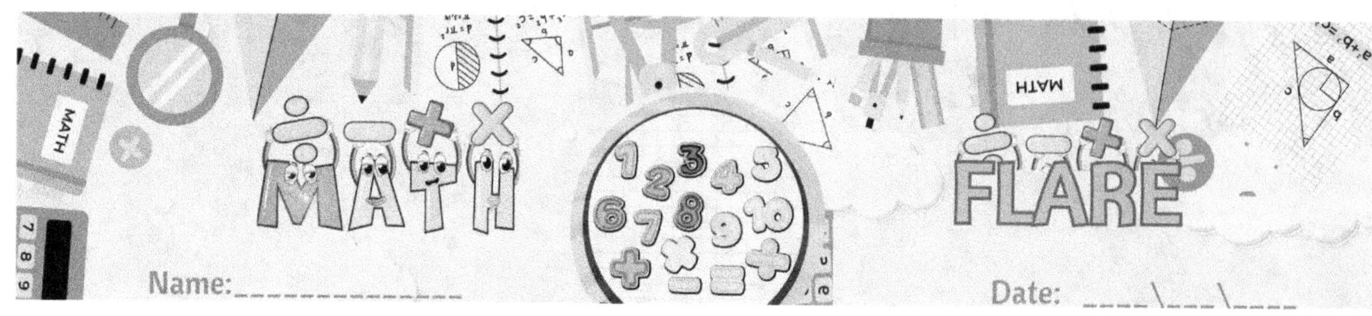

291. You have 396 bandages and want to share them equally with six people. How many bandages would each person get?

292. A roll of tape is 40 feet long. If Brooklyn needs to cut the tape into five pieces that are all the same length, how long will each piece be?

293. Luke read a book that had 640 pages in 10 days. If he read the same number of pages each day, how many pages did he read per day?

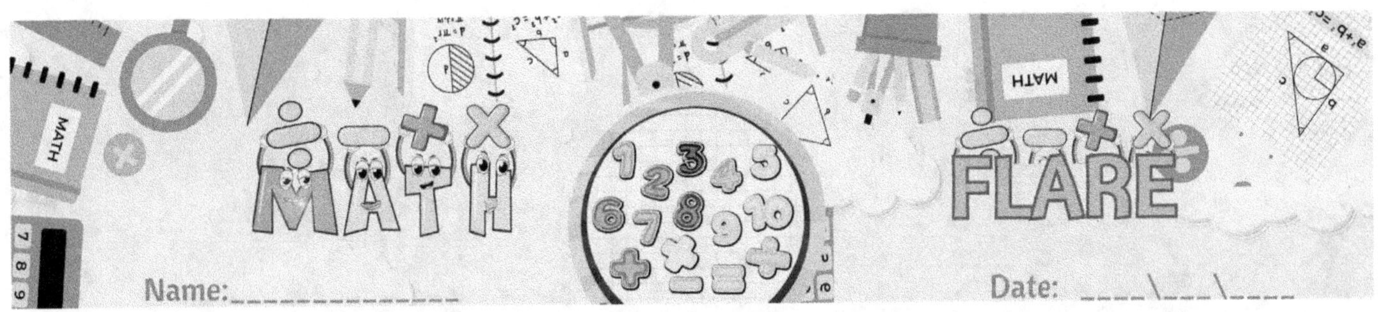

294. Ryder drove 144 miles in eight hours. What was Ryder's average speed in miles per hour?

295. If a field is 675 acres and it is divided into nine equal parts, how many acres is each part?

296. Sophia is filling up water bottles. Each bottle holds four ounces of water. If Sophia has 244 ounces of water, how many water bottles can she fill up?

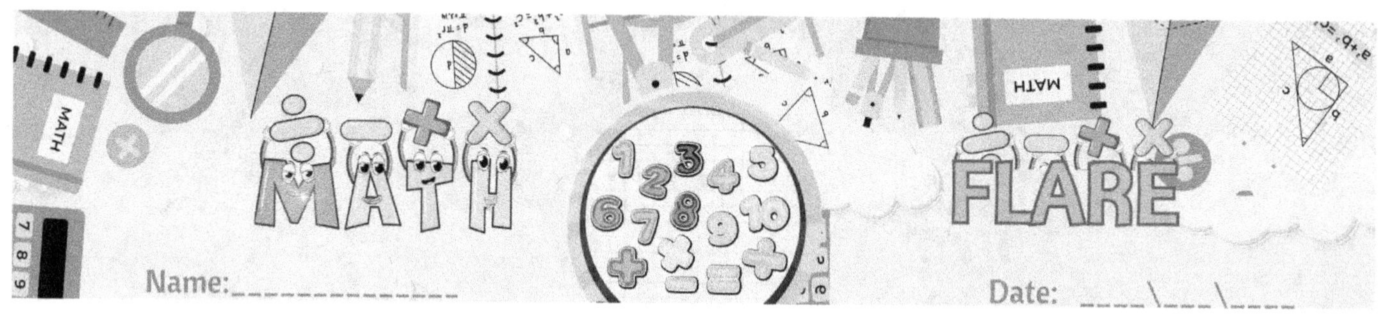

297. A recipe calls for 44 cups of sugar to make two cookies. How much sugar is needed to make 1 cookie?

298. Grace has 820 watches and wants to divide them equally among 10 people. How many watches will each person get?

299. If a garden is 35 feet long and it is divided into seven equal parts, how long is each part?

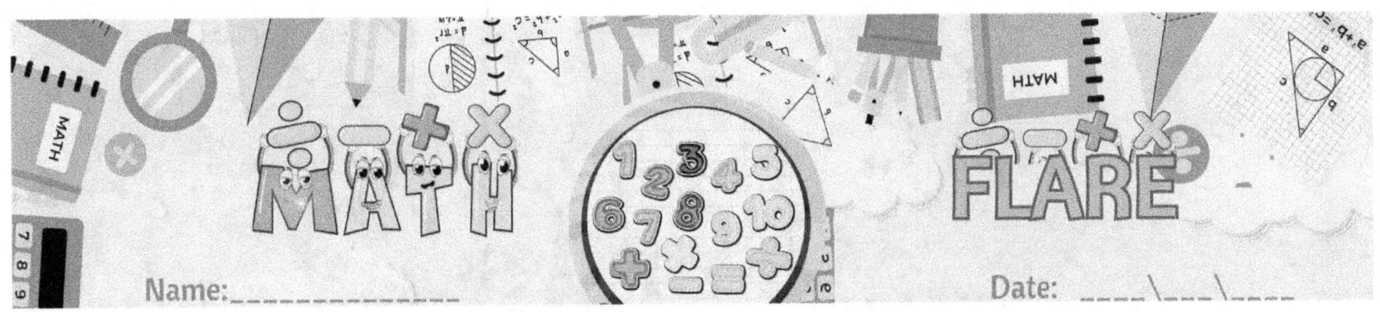

300. A box of soaps has 40 soaps. If 20 children each get an equal number of soaps, how many soaps will each child get?

301. If Jordyn has 77 pens and wants to distribute them equally to 11 students, how many pens will each student get?

302. Diego is reading a book with 1,027 pages. If Diego wants to read the same number of pages every day, how many pages would Diego have to read each day to finish in 13 days?

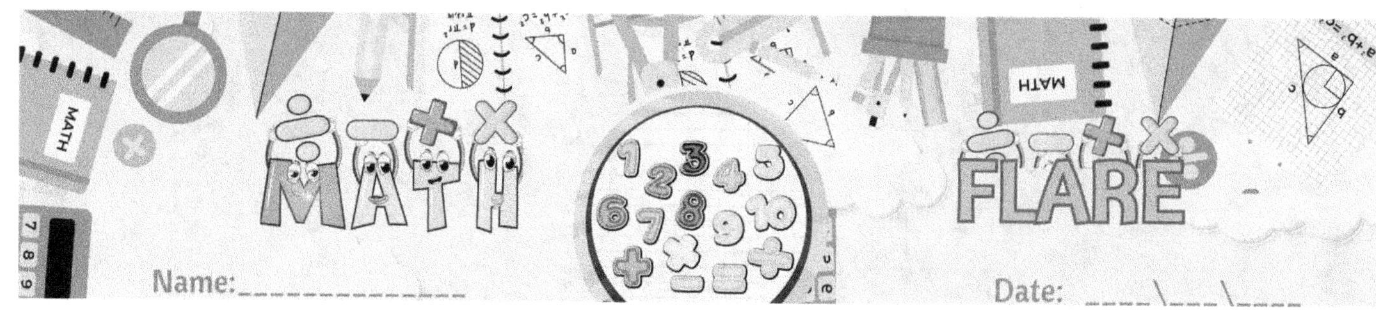

303. If Asher has 10 coins and wants to share them equally among five friends, how many coins will each friend get?

304. Nicholas has 240 dollars and wants to buy five cookies. How much can he spend on each cookies?

305. Isabelle made 320 cookies for a bake sale. She put the cookies in bags, with 20 cookies in each bag. How many bags did she have for the bake sale?

306. If a garden is 792 feet wide and it is divided into 12 equal parts, how wide is each part?

307. How many five cm pieces of pipe can you cut from a pipe that is 185 cm long?

308. Naomi has 776 perfumes and wants to divide them equally among eight children. How many perfumes will each child get?

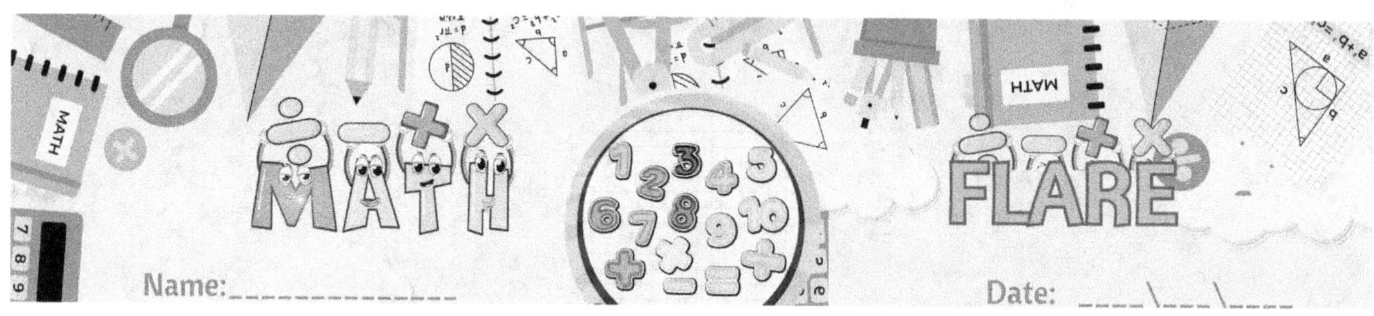

309. A rope is 480 meters long. If you cut it into 12 equal pieces, how long is each piece?

310. Christian has 350 pages of homework to do. If he wants to finish his homework in 10 days, how many pages does he need to do each day?

311. Amelia bought five carrots for a total of $80. How much did each carrots cost?

ANSWERS

Page 1: Multi Digit Multiplication

1. 20,297,592	2. 47,601,756	3. 8,261,603	4. 9,159,704
5. 9,711,954	6. 18,105,578	7. 14,751,372	8. 22,836,634
9. 15,556,860	10. 82,048,120	11. 37,997,580	12. 44,684,768
13. 53,879,448	14. 52,142,840	15. 51,846,115	16. 5,202,210
17. 6,960,448	18. 3,292,437	19. 56,338,900	20. 28,950,642
21. 12,288,580	22. 13,020,145	23. 3,965,976	24. 12,903,196
25. 41,803,969	26. 26,526,094	27. 32,813,550	28. 42,298,641
29. 69,845,482	30. 30,297,267	31. 43,491,942	32. 27,504,288
33. 13,925,371	34. 51,871,490	35. 17,854,452	36. 3,329,025
37. 24,176,064	38. 21,454,080	39. 20,695,602	40. 22,210,288
41. 13,580,996	42. 6,413,344	43. 19,614,384	44. 27,867,028
45. 37,619,400	46. 27,497,742	47. 46,359,318	48. 15,319,766
49. 48,949,120	50. 9,790,464	51. 42,229,044	52. 19,582,524
53. 21,080,565	54. 56,123,305	55. 23,419,382	56. 11,319,220
57. 52,683,815	58. 55,018,934	59. 13,368,116	60. 25,656,026
61. 66,481,117	62. 6,359,030	63. 50,097,096	

Page 8: Long Division

64. 4,574.7	65. 1,823.9	66. 4,528	67. 30,459	68. 15,587.5
69. 5,155.1	70. 10,395	71. 1,909.6	72. 17,631	73. 2,348.8

74. 1,613.7   75. 9,678.4   76. 2,183.9   77. 7,411.7   78. 23,828

79. 1,362.9   80. 4,069.1   81. 18,086   82. 8,005.9   83. 7,915.8

84. 3,506.5   85. 3,124.1   86. 6,948.7   87. 4,719.8   88. 1,931

89. 12,126.7   90. 9,061.6   91. 4,785.2   92. 3,924.2   93. 30,505.7

94. 13,132.4   95. 5,248.3   96. 24,826.8   97. 2,132   98. 9,163

99. 9,468   100. 3,401.3   101. 10,437.9   102. 5,827.4   103. 5,183.2

104. 4,476.4   105. 1,031.1   106. 18,881   107. 2,306.6   108. 8,801.3

109. 3,677.7   110. 3,825.4   111. 6,196.8

Page 16: Long Division: Remainders

112. 21,227 R38   113. 23,647 R7   114. 4,901 R35

115. 15,517 R19   116. 23,313 R27   117. 5,967 R22

118. 10,741 R39   119. 31,134 R30   120. 21,659 R3

121. 16,714 R47   122. 29,920 R5   123. 64,847 R12

124. 27,449 R11   125. 2,691 R1   126. 16,888 R0

127. 75,535 R9   128. 9,219 R10   129. 27,294 R10

130. 14,979 R36   131. 47,923 R16   132. 11,360 R6

133. 42,245 R11   134. 12,998 R1   135. 8,176 R0

136. 3,168 R39   137. 37,944 R8   138. 33,983 R8

139. 9,132 R9   140. 40,513 R10   141. 16,353 R22

142. 24,884 R35   143. 5,174 R19   144. 44,795 R11

145. 49,602 R12   146. 13,259 R14   147. 40,675 R10

148. 5,391 R15

149. 51,922 R4

150. 2,171 R43

151. 46,138 R9

152. 7,052 R29

153. 22,208 R30

154. 29,721 R25

155. 6,111 R18

156. 20,346 R5

157. 17,235 R7

158. 19,953 R5

159. 9,833 R23

160. 20,209 R29

161. 36,163 R11

162. 11,480 R2

163. 33,258 R8

164. 4,176 R29

165. 16,409 R17

166. 57,957 R13

167. 10,222 R28

168. 14,407 R1

169. 52,350 R7

170. 33,002 R13

171. 58,793 R11

172. 6,916 R15

173. 5,219 R12

174. 14,601 R5

175. 20,521 R5

176. 7,616 R44

177. 17,446 R21

178. 13,364 R35

179. 33,332 R20

180. 6,924 R9

181. 41,536 R17

182. 6,515 R34

183. 16,636 R1

184. 22,439 R6

185. 3,045 R4

186. 25,633 R17

187. 43,099 R0

188. 36,253 R9

189. 6,294 R21

190. 43,831 R11

191. 28,623 R10

Page 36: Using the Power of 10

192. 80.00

193. 900.0

194. 300.0

195. 300

196. 90,000

197. 200,000

198. 30.00

199. 70

200. 600.0

201. 70

202. 50,000

203. 80,000

204. 1

205. 600,000

206. 200,000

207. 9,000,000

208. 2

209. 40,000

210. 100,000

211. 1,000,000

212. 30.00   213. 50   214. 400.0   215. 400,000

216. 60.00   217. 900,000   218. 50   219. 500.0

220. 7,000,000   221. 7   222. 60.00   223. 70,000

224. 8,000,000   225. 9,000,000   226. 300,000   227. 90

228. 30,000   229. 400   230. 100.0   231. 50.00

232. 60.00   233. 700,000   234. 60,000   235. 100,000

236. 90,000   237. 400   238. 10.00   239. 500,000

240. 40,000   241. 80,000   242. 3,000,000   243. 400,000

244. 700,000   245. 200,000   246. 40   247. 30,000

248. 500,000   249. 80,000   250. 600   251. 900

Page 41: Multiplication Word Problems

252. 52   253. 56   254. 18   255. 228   256. 252   257. 78   258. 198

259. 76   260. 221   261. 50   262. 180   263. 84   264. 26   265. 180

266. 152   267. 16   268. 108   269. 108   270. 51   271. 180   272. 380

273. 187   274. 63   275. 110   276. 49   277. 10   278. 39   279. 39

280. 221   281. 208

Page 51: Division Word Problems

282. 87   283. 52   284. 27   285. 66   286. 189   287. 3   288. 47

289. 43   290. 47   291. 66   292. 8   293. 64   294. 18   295. 75

296. 61   297. 22   298. 82   299. 5   300. 2   301. 7   302. 79

303. 2   304. 48   305. 16   306. 66   307. 37   308. 97   309. 40

310. 35   311. 16